*PICTURE FRAMING*

MAX HYDER

# PICTURE FRAMING

*Photography by Ted Davies*

BONANZA BOOKS · NEW YORK

0-517-010747

© MCMLXIII Pitman Publishing Corporation. All rights reserved. No part of this book may be reproduced in any form without the written permission of the publisher. Library of Congress Catalog Card Number: 63—15302. Designed by Stefan Salter. Printed in the United States of America. 1.98765432

This edition published by Bonanza Books,
a division of Crown Publishers, Inc.,
by arrangement with Pitman Publishing Corporation
      e  f  g  h

# FOREWORD

This little book sets forth basic rules and procedures for simple picture framing. Artists and home craftsmen who wish to make frames with materials and tools available to everyone will find these pages helpful. Even those who do not plan to construct their own frames will gain a familiarity with the subject that will enable them to deal more knowledgeably with professional framers.

# CONTENTS

*PICTURE FRAMING*

# BASIC CONSIDERATIONS

The frame has always been an important element in the display of works of art. Complete integration may at once be seen in Gothic and early Renaissance frames. To remove the frame from, say, the Lorenzo di Bicci reproduced here would be to destroy almost half the merit of the piece. Many early masterpieces lose much of the spirit of their times when deprived of their richly ornamented and overwrought frames. This book does not deal with anything so complex as the elaborately carved and gilded frames illustrated here. A valuable work is best framed by a professional.

Unknown Florentine painter: *Coronation of the Virgin and Saints* (1394), Triptich 78″ x 76″ over-all. The Metropolitan Museum of Art, gift of Robert Lehman, 1950.

Lorenzo di Bicci: *Madonna and Child with Saint Matthew and Saint Francis* (c. 1400), 45″ x 23½″ over-all. The Metropolitan Museum of Art, gift of George Blumenthal, 1941.

In choosing a frame for a specific work of art keep in mind these basic ideas: A picture should not be *overframed*; the frame should not command more attention than the picture. This does not necessarily mean that all picture frames should be simple. It does mean that the frame must be so integrated with the work of art that it becomes a part of it. While it is true that many modern pictures require little in the way of framing, others need more. And in framing traditional styles of art, we can take hints from earlier generations by visiting museums to observe how various kinds of paintings and drawings have been framed in other periods.

The first and most important consideration for the framer is the proper *weight* of frame for the piece he is framing, because the bulk of the frame must complement the size and composition in the artwork itself. I have generally found that the smaller the painting, the larger the frame it requires. For small panels, enamels, or tiles I have often used frames twice or three times the width of the piece, particularly if the design is bold.

Large paintings can usually be framed pleasingly with narrow molding—especially in the case of modern canvases, many of which approach mural proportions. These often look best with nothing more than a stripping along the edge to cover the tacks and unpainted canvas.

Most abstract paintings look best in *flat* frames or stripping—a thin wooden slat perhaps ¼″ × 1½″ tacked *on edge* around the outside of the canvas stretcher, defining the picture's limits in a neat, thin line. Many artists use ordinary lath or lattice strips and paint them black, white, or gray. More expensive stripping is of mahogany or walnut, often with the edge (or *face*) gilded to create the effect of a gold or silver band around the picture. Stripping must be flat both on the face and on the side (or *back*).

Angular frame constructed of beveled moldings—one forward, one reverse. Such a frame would emphasize angularity in the picture.

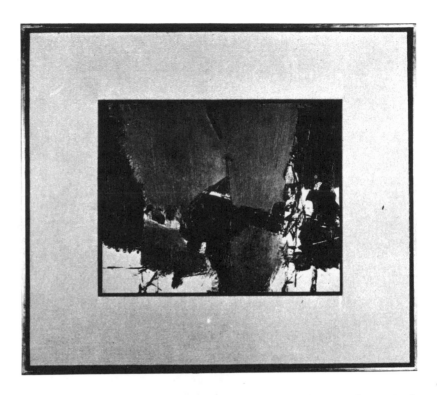

Budd Hopkins: *Study for Lafayette,* 11″ x 14″ panel, frame and mat 4½″.

For smaller abstract pieces, however, stripping alone may look insignificant. Adding a mat to enlarge the piece and create a *breathing area* between it and the stripping may enhance the effect. The mat may be covered with linen or other fabric. The illustration on this page shows a small painting so treated. The picture (11″ x 14″) was *flush-mounted* in a linen mat 4 inches wide.

*Flush mounting* means that the art is placed in a mat or liner so that its surface is even with the surface of the mat. (This method usually entails more problems than the use of traditional mountings, which overlap the edges of the framed piece.) Flush mounting is often desirable, however, when a major element of the composition falls so near the edge that even a ⅛″ overlap may be critical.

Almost all pictures look better if framed first in some kind of liner

Very wide frame used on a very small picture. Petrus Christus: *Portrait of a Carthusian* (c. 1450), 11½″ x 8″ panel, frame 5½″. The Metropolitan Museum of Art, the Jules S. Bache Collection, 1949.

Deep scoop used to create an air of intimacy. Joseph Granata: *Monk*, 10″ x 14″ panel, frame 3½″.

or mounting before being placed within the actual molding of an outside frame. Even a very small line of black, white, or gold circling the edge heightens visual effectiveness of the finished work. The width of this element in the frame should be judged by both the size of the picture and the frame you intend to place around it. For a small picture you may wish to use a wide (or *heavy*) frame with a narrow (*light*) liner. If the frame molding is to be 4″ wide, the liner should not exceed ¾″. Conversely, if a 4″ liner or mat is used, it should be surrounded by a ¾″ frame. In any case, the effect to be avoided is that of equal weight—for example, never use a 1½″ liner with a 1½″ frame.

William Trost Richards: *Surf on Rocks,* 8¾″ x 15⅞″ panel, frame 2½″. The Metropolitan Museum of Art, gift of Mrs. William T. Brewster, 1932.

The shape of the molding is another important consideration. Having determined the proper weight and proportion for the frame and liner, you will find that different shapes of moldings can subtly reflect certain qualities of the picture. A composition with rounded forms and soft volumes may be enhanced by a curved molding; one with sharp lines and jagged shapes may look best in a more angular molding.

A deep *scoop* shape may add an air of intimacy to a small interior or a close-up portrait; the expanse of a seascape may need a wide, simple shape. A more detailed discussion of this aspect of framing will be found on pages 26–32.

Piet Mondrian: *Composition 2* (1922), 21⅞″ x 21⅛″ canvas, frame 3″. The Solomon R. Guggenheim Museum.

Type of finish is also important to a successful framing job. The most elementary finishes take advantage of the natural qualities of the moldings used.

Picture-frame moldings are available in a variety of woods. The most common and least expensive are *basswood*, the white grainless wood of the linden tree. When basswood is evenly colored, it is often left natural and simply given a wax finish. Basswood can be stained to harmonize with the painting. For instance, a picture with rich oranges and browns might look good on a white mat in a frame with a fruitwood or maple stain, which would echo and accent the oranges and browns in the composition. A picture with cool greens and blues would look better in a walnut-stained frame.

To paint a frame an actual color such as orange or green is not usually a good idea. Brightly colored frames tend to compete with the picture, so that the frame becomes the decorative element. To be sure, this effect *can* be used successfully; many interior decorators hang groupings of small prints with frames colored to match, for instance, rug or drapes. But we are concerned here primarily with framing as an *art*, and we do not wish the frame to detract from the picture.

Some moldings are made of *wormy chestnut*, which has a pleasing natural texture and a color suitable for framing works that require a rustic look—landscapes, flora and fauna. Natural walnut and mahogany are also used as molding materials, and these are handsome.

The most common *painted* finishes are white, antique white, and black. They are used primarily to hide less-desirable molding materials such as pine or fir. Many of the popular lumber shapes are available only in such woods. A few years ago the white frame was widely acclaimed, and it is still often used, especially for purist abstract pictures. The crisp lines and clean spaces of a Mondrian seem to demand nothing more than a stark, smooth white. This kind of finish, however, does not age gracefully. Pure-white paint yellows in a short time and, of course, every finger mark or smudge mars its pristine quality.

Various *antique-white* finishes can be produced by several different means. Generally this finish consists of a basic white frame that has been intentionally discolored to a buff or gray. These moldings are often suitable for watercolors and brightly colored prints or reproductions. They

Antique-white frame used to advantage on a traditional still life. The liner is in an almost-pure white for contrast. Lillian Lagana: *Still Life*, 16″ x 20″ canvas, frame 3″.

are more durable than pure-white frames and less expensive than those with metallic finishes.

This is a good point to mention antiquing and distressing, two terms frequently used in framing. *Antiquing* usually refers to a coating applied over the finish of a frame to make it appear less new, to give it a softer, mellower, more middle-toned quality. According to individual taste, the workman antiques with or without *distressing*, artificial wear or damage. Framers distress by scratching with a wire brush or sharp instrument, by rasping, or by striking with a tool. These effects are carried to perfection by some professionals, who fake antique frames for museums to replace unsuitable authentic ones. Most frames of high quality are antiqued to some degree.

Black frames are sometimes useful, but they should never be too wide. Small black frames not more than ½″ wide are effective for matted prints, photographs, drawings, etchings, and the like.

Bright metallic effects are seldom pleasing except to cover such small areas as the edge of stripping, a liner, or the face of a frame less than ½″ wide. Any larger gilded surfaces should be softened.

Good taste in framing is like good taste in any other area; it is partly native and partly learned. The best combinations can be achieved only through practice and observation—by testing your own results with a critical eye and by observing how others have solved similar problems.

Max Hyder: *St. Francis of Assisi*, 10″ x 10½″ serigraph, mat and frame 2½″ x 3″.

# BASIC MOLDING PROFILES

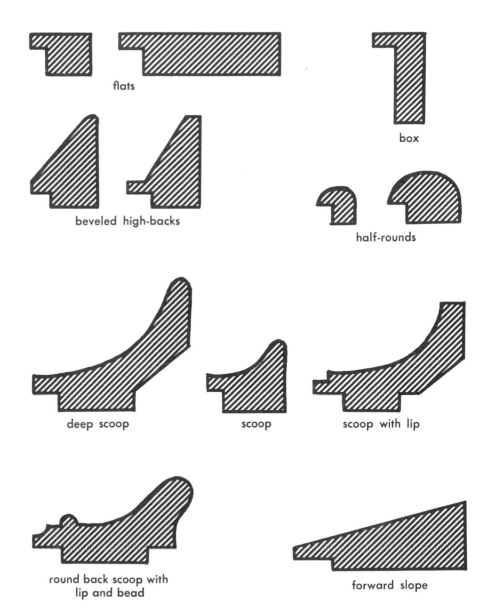

flats

box

beveled high-backs

half-rounds

deep scoop

scoop

scoop with lip

round back scoop with
lip and bead

forward slope

Cross-section profiles of actual picture-frame moldings, available in many lumberyards and building-supply houses. Large quantities and a much wider variety of shapes are available from picture-frame molding suppliers, on a wholesale basis only.

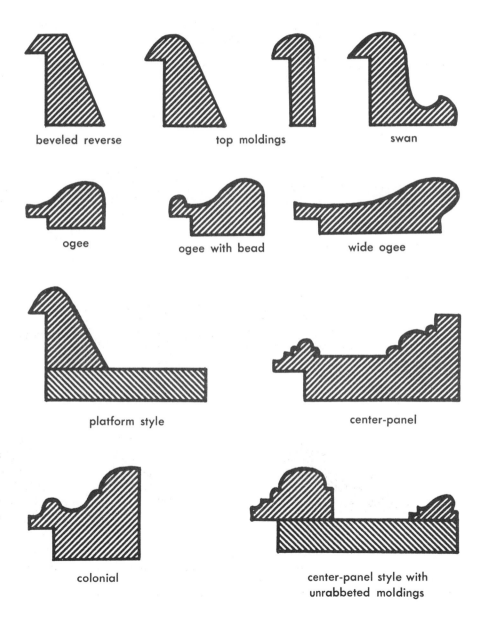

beveled reverse

top moldings

swan

ogee

ogee with bead

wide ogee

platform style

center-panel

colonial

center-panel style with
unrabbeted moldings

# LUMBER TRADE MOLDINGS

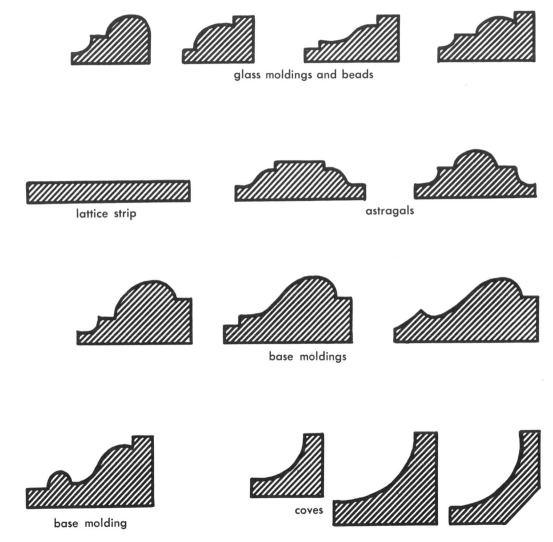

glass moldings and beads

lattice strip

astragals

base moldings

base molding

coves

Unrabbeted moldings intended for purposes other than picture framing. These can be readily adapted to framing by using them in combination with flat planks and slats to create a great variety of frames. The styles most easily made from such moldings are the *platform* and the *center-panel,* since both consist of a wide flat

24

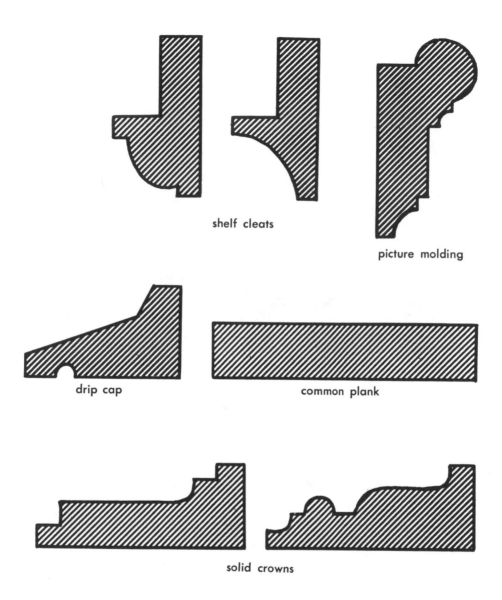

shelf cleats

picture molding

drip cap

common plank

solid crowns

piece to which raised moldings are attached. The *rabbet* is formed by allowing the molding nearest the picture to project over the edge of the flat piece, providing a groove to receive the picture. (These styles may also be created, of course, with standard rabbeted moldings.) The *flat* or plain plank frame is cut first, large enough to receive the picture. The molding to go next to the picture is measured by the inside edge of the flat frame, allowing it to project over the edge ¼" to form the rabbet. The outside molding is cut to fit snugly around the flat at its outside edge.

25

Byzantine icon, artist unknown: *The Virgin of the Sign* (17th century), 12¼″ x 10½″ over-all. The Metropolitan Museum of Art, gift of Mrs. Henry Morgenthau, 1933.

# KINDS AND STYLES
# OF FRAMES

The most ancient and basic of all frames is the simple *flat*, from which the more complex styles evolved. In the early Byzantine use of the flat in icons, the frame is nothing more than a raised border around the painted area. This was not even a *frame*, strictly speaking—it was merely the edge of the painting panel itself, the area for the picture having been scooped out to a depth of perhaps ¼″. By the time of Giotto (died 1337) it had

Girolamo Da Cremona (1467–1483): *Descent from the Cross*, 6¼″ x 4½″, frame 2½″.
The Metropolitan Museum of Art, the Jules S. Bache Collection, 1949.

Traditional use of the railroad frame on a panel of modest dimensions. The finish is gold leaf with painted designs in colors from the painting. Bartolomeo di Tommaso da Foligno (1425–1455): *Lamentation and Entombment*. The Metropolitan Museum of Art, Gwynne M. Andrews Fund, 1958.

become separate from the artwork panel and was often decorated with painted, incised, or tool-stamped designs. In the early Renaissance it took the form now called the *railroad* frame: a flat panel with a small raised edge on each side—a style still widely used.

The *center-panel* and the *platform* styles, obvious developments of the railroad frame, became the most popular frames of the Renaissance; both are still in wide use. For a modern example of the platform frame, see the Clawson *Façade* (page 29), which is framed in a simple rolled-back top molding mounted on a wide driftwood flat.

These frames are easily constructed from materials available in most lumberyards, and the possibilities for decoration are almost endless. The top molding and outside edge are often leafed in gold or silver. The

Typical modern use of the platform frame. The cross-section drawing (page 30, top) illustrates construction. The rounded top molding has been attached to the flat back molding by glue and by nails driven from the back side. The top molding is gold, the back molding driftwood. Rex Clawson: *Façade*, 18″ x 26″ canvas, frame 5″.

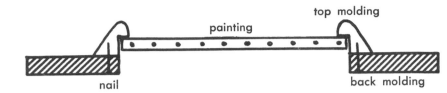

top molding

painting

nail

back molding

center panel or flat back may be toned to appropriate colors to go with the painting (see "Materials and Methods for Finishing," p. 59).

*Driftwood* effects are often used, especially with platform-style framing; sometimes the flat is covered with fabric, such as linen or velvet, or with a tortoise-shell or other paper. A favorite Renaissance effect was the use of *graffito*—a painted pattern done over gold-leafed surfaces. Graffito was usually done in black—lampblack in japan is good for this purpose. The designs were usually scrollwork, floral pattern, or lettering. The illustration on page 27 is an example of a center-panel style with graffito work. This kind of decoration can be done with japan colors over metal-leaf surfaces. The frame should then be shellacked and *antiqued*.

The platform frame during the Renaissance often had a large, richly carved and gilded *top molding* and a back molding painted black, maroon, or some other dark color. In recent years there has been a simplification of the form in which the top molding is plain, often merely painted white although sometimes gilded; the back molding is usually finished in driftwood or left natural if the plank is of chestnut, walnut, or some other handsome wood.

The most recent variation of the platform style is merely a flat stripping mounted edgewise on a flat back. This kind of frame is used on the Mondrian work reproduced earlier. It is especially suitable for pictures on which an overlapping rabbet would cover part of the composition.

For centuries the Chinese have used a variation of the flat frame known as the *ogee*. The profile presents a gentle S curve with the high

Ogee profiles.

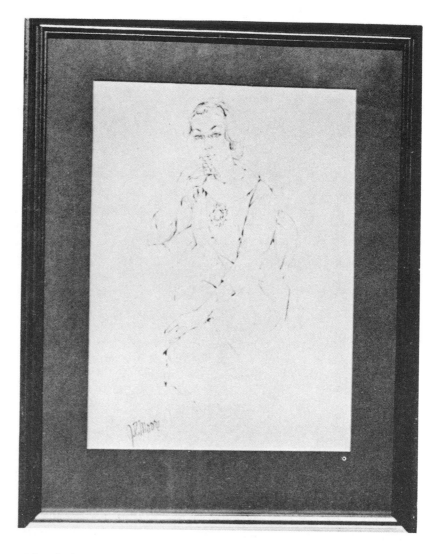

Colonial shape in antique-silver finish used with a mat and glass to frame a drawing. Robert Moore: *Drawing*, 14″ x 18″, frame and mat 3″ x 3½″.

ridge at the outside—the inside face is scooped out and rounded into a soft curve. This style has wide application, especially for Oriental works.

Many early American paintings need little more than a simple forward-slope frame, a gently beveled style that resembles the often-homemade frames of Colonial times. These usually look best in natural wood—maple or antique pine—especially for framing the more primitive types of early American art.

More sophisticated work, including such things as the famous British hunting prints, go well in the frame shape known as *Colonial*, which is similar to the ogee but with more exaggeration to the curve. Available in a great many sizes, this molding is usually finished in antique metallic effects—most frequently *antique silver*. (This finish consists of an aluminum-leafed face with *gold lacquer* passed along the *cove* section to add a warm glow. There are also usually spatterings of black *flyspecks*.) The *back* or outside edge is almost invariably painted black. This frame makes a handsome setting for drawings and prints of all periods.

Two other popular frame styles are *box* moldings and *reverse bevels*. The box is actually a flat, deeper (or wider) on the back than on the face, commonly ½″ wide by 1″ or 1½″ deep. *Reverse-bevel* molding resembles the box except that the back or side slopes at an angle toward the wall. Both shapes are available in a variety of woods and are beautiful with simple wax finishes. The face is sometimes gilded. The example on page 33 is a walnut reverse bevel with a gold face.

Sr. Mary Corita, IHM: *Genesis VI,* 8½" x 28" serigraph, frame and mat 3". Courtesy Dr. M. Mycek.

# MEASURING

There are two broad classifications of picture frame: those which use glass and those which do not. In the final section of this book each of the two framing processes is described, step by step. At this point we will consider the components and the methods used to determine measurements.

The article under glass—usually a watercolor, a drawing, an original print, a reproduction, a stone rubbing, or a photograph—often requires a *mat*—a border made of paper, fabric, or other material all around the piece *within the actual picture frame*. To arrive at the proper measurements for the frame you must first decide on the size of the mat.

The most common mats are of paper matboard obtainable from art-supply stores. Numerous colors and textures are available, but the majority of matting jobs employ white or off-white boards in smooth or eggshell finish. The so-called *pebble* finish is also widely used, but usually is esthetically less satisfying. For framing delicate original works of art there are available boards made of rag paper which will not yellow with age and are unlikely to leave acid stain on the border of the artwork.

Standard matboard is sold in 30″ × 40″ sheets. *Double-thick* board is also produced. Double-thick board produces a wider *bevel* when the mat is cut; it is also best for making mats that are to be covered with fabric.

To determine desirable mat width, lay the artwork on a sheet of matboard and hold a piece of the molding you intend to use at varying distances from the picture until you arrive at a satisfying proportion between picture, mat width, and molding weight. Some works need very little mat surface, particularly those with large white areas within the picture. Other pieces look best with very wide mats. The average mat for, say, a 14″ × 18″ picture will usually be 2½″ to 3″. If the picture is post-card size, 5″ or 6″ may be desirable. The mat should not duplicate too closely the width or height of the artwork. There should be at least an inch of difference, larger or smaller. If you are framing a large piece (say 24″ × 30″), a 2″ or 2½″ mat may suffice.

In measuring for the mat and in making all other measurements, use a standard folding rule calibrated in eighth-inches; smaller measurements are not practical in picture framing. The folding rule is 6′ long, enabling you to make any measurement in one span.

To calculate the over-all size of the mat, once you have decided on the all-around width, you must establish an *opening* size. (The opening is the *window* in the mat through which the work will be seen.) The opening should be large enough to display almost all of the artwork, but not so large as to expose the edges of the paper.

Measure slightly *inside* the picture area: if the picture area is exactly 11″ × 14″, the opening must not be more than 10¾″ × 13¾″ to

Using the folding rule to measure for the mat.

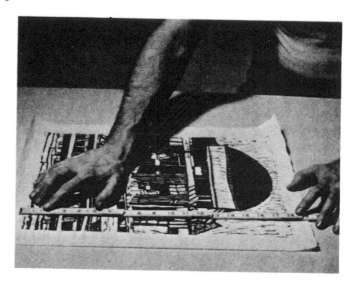

Drawing the mat opening, using T square and rule.

allow for an ⅛″ covering all around. If the picture is one which cannot afford this loss of area, consider the *drop-on mounting* discussed below. In framing original etchings, woodcuts, lithographs, serigraphs, or similar prints it is customary to leave ¼″ to ½″ of the printing paper showing around the printed image; for etchings the border should be sufficient to expose the plate marks. This *floating border* allows the artist's signature and the print-edition numbers (usually just below the picture) to remain visible—one reason the border is often wider at the bottom.

Having established the window size, add the mat width to it. Thus, if the opening is to be 10¾″ × 13¾″ and the mat 3″ wide, add 6″ to each dimension, making the over-all size 16¾″ × 19¾″. For a vertical picture you may wish to extend the mat slightly at the bottom, perhaps ½″ more; the size would then be 16¾″ × 20¼″. (Most horizontal pictures look best if the matting is even all around.) This outside dimension is now used to measure the frame.

After cutting a piece of matboard to the proper size, draw the shape of the window on it using a T square and rule.

Frames that do not use glass pose a slightly different problem in measuring. These frames are usually intended to receive canvases or panels and are not cut so close to the actual measurement as are those in which glass will be used. In measuring for a canvas, add ¼″ allowance to the actual size. Give panels only ⅛″ allowance. *Allowance* is the term for the amount of play or extra room in the rabbet of a frame to accommodate glass, panel, or canvas with ease. Nothing should ever be forced into too tight a frame. Even if the piece fits at first, expansion and contraction are sure to cause later problems. Canvases require the largest allowance because they are seldom absolutely square; the tacking along the edge also protrudes beyond the actual stretcher size. Many large moldings (3″ and up) have an extra-large rabbet because these frames are most often used for canvases. Commercially cut panels are usually more true and thus require less allowance. The allowance in a frame that is to receive glass is usually quite small—just enough to be sure the measurement is full.

The cross section of a picture-frame molding (page 37) makes clear why measurements should be made along the *back* of the rabbet—the part that will actually encompass the picture (the front of the painting will rest against the lip which keeps it from coming through the frame).

Framers often use the term *sight-size* to specify the measurement of the portion of a picture that is actually visible from the front of the frame. If the lip of the rabbet is ¼″ wide, the actual opening in the frame will be ½″ less than the measurement made along the back of the rabbet. Thus a frame cut exactly 16″ × 20″ will expose only 15½″ × 19½″ of the picture, the frame's *sight-size*.

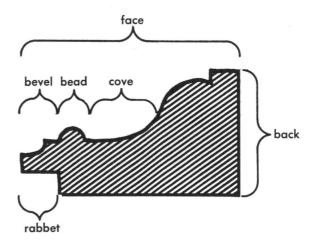

Cross section of a typical picture-frame molding.

# MOUNTS, LINERS, AND MATS

## MOUNTS

Many small things—painted panels, enamels, ceramic tiles, medallions, and similar objects—are best framed without glass after being set in a *mount*. The mount will vary with the requirements of the object, but many things can be set into a heavy mat cut from 3/16″ Upson board, a thick builder's cardboard available in 4′ × 8′ sheets from lumber suppliers. It is easily cut with the mat knife by simply drawing the blade repeatedly through the original cut until the whole thickness has been penetrated. Do not try to cut it with one stroke by applying pressure. Double-thick matboard, which is thick enough for some purposes, should be cut in the same manner.

In the example shown on page 39, a small panel was laid on a piece of Upson board already cut to allow a border all around. The piece was centered carefully, using a rule. A line was drawn around the panel; then, using straight edge and mat knife, the opening was cut straight down just outside the line. (It was necessary to cut outside the line to allow room for the thickness of the fabric—red velvet—with which the mount was covered.) Another piece of Upson board was cut to serve as backing and was painted black to prevent its showing around the edges of the mounted piece. The backing was glued to the mount and the panel was glued in place. The entire mount, panel in place, was then nailed into the frame.

## LINERS

*Liner* is the term used for the small flat or beveled molding that frames a canvas or panel inside a larger frame. It creates a line around the piece and separates the color and tone of the picture from that of the frame, making the transition less abrupt. This little space of neutral color allows the painting to *breathe*, so that it neither competes with nor melts into the color of the frame.

Harry Sternberg: *Napoleon Brandy,* 5″ x 7″ panel, frame and mount 3″ x 3½″.
Courtesy A.C.A. Gallery.

Liner molding usually has a rabbet. The visible surface is often covered with linen, velvet, or other material. When not covered, it is ordinarily painted—gray, beige, white, or black—or is leafed in gold or silver. Liners are cut exactly as other frames. The procedure for covering a liner with fabric is the same as that for covering a mat.

## MATS

We have already discussed how to measure a mat and how to draw the shape for the window; let us now proceed to cut and cover a mat. (Not all mats are covered, of course, but they are all cut in the same manner.)

Lay the mat on the cutting table with a strip of scrap matboard underneath the first line you intend to cut; this provides a cushion the knife can penetrate without damaging the table. Place the steel straightedge approximately ⅛″ away from the line toward the outside of the mat. You may wish to C-clamp the end of the straightedge to the table to hold it firmly in place. Insert the mat knife blade at about a 45° angle, resting the edge of the blade against the steel edge. Pull the knife along steadily and smoothly, trying to maintain the same blade angle the full length of the cut. Regular matboard should cut through with one pass of the knife, leaving a good clean bevel. Double-thick matboard and Upson board may require three or more passes over the same cut.

When all four sides have been cut, the center should lift out readily. Ragged edges on the bevel can usually be removed by sandpapering lightly on the reverse side with fine sandpaper.

Several kinds of mat knives are available in hardware and art-supply stores. The one shown here is a Stanley No. 199, which has changeable blades stored in the handle. To cut good mats the knife must be very sharp.

After cutting the mat, cut a piece of *backing* board to use behind the picture and mat in the frame. This can be made of gray *chipboard*, which is cheaper than matboard. Many framers use ordinary corrugated

liner          painting          frame

Cross section of a typical frame with liner.

Hold the knife firmly and try to maintain the same angle the entire length of the cut.

board; the sides of used cartons are satisfactory. If you are framing an expensive work of art or a somewhat transparent piece, place a sheet of white drawing paper behind the work before the backing is put in place.

### Hinged Mats

Many times the hinged mat (also called *folder mat*) will be useful, for example when pieces are being matted and not framed. Even for pieces that are to be framed it is an added protection. As can be seen, the folder mat is formed by simply attaching a second sheet of matboard to the back of the mat with a gummed-paper hinge. The art work is then tipped lightly in place on the backing and the mat brought down on top. For attaching the artwork, small hinges cut from white gummed-paper tape or dabs of library paste work well. When a hinged mat is not used most framers attach the artwork to the back of the mat with bits of masking tape at the corners and centers of the sides. (Do not run the tape all around the edges—buckling will result.)

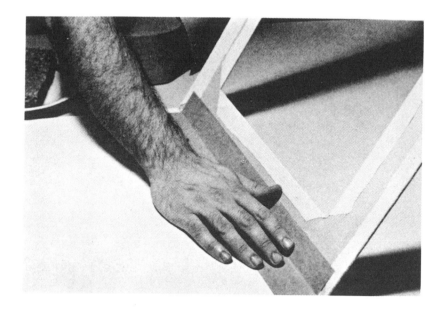

Placing gummed-tape hinge between mat and back.

*Covered Mats*

Most pictures are enhanced by the use of an appropriate fabric or textured covering on the mat or liner. By far the commonest material currently used is linen—in natural or white. This can be purchased by the yard from any dress-goods store. Try to get linen of medium to heavy weave; too fine a texture will be ineffective. White is better if slightly off-white, and natural if it tends more to gray-beige than to tan. Avoid pinkish tones. Some people prefer monk's cloth, burlap, grasscloth, or velvet to linen for covering.

For velvet-covered mats or liners, cotton-backed velvets are the most satisfactory. Use a stiff clothes brush to brush the pile in one direction before putting the piece aside to dry.

Once you have selected the proper fabric, it must be glued to the mat or liner. A white casein glue such as Elmer's Glue-all is excellent for this purpose. Lay the fabric, cut an inch or more larger than the piece to be covered, face down on the table. Cover the entire mat or liner surface with glue, using a stiff brush and spreading evenly. Be careful not to

42

leave puddles that may penetrate the fabric and cause glue spots. Turn the glue-coated surface face down onto the fabric, first making certain the fabric is stretched smooth. Apply pressure all around with the hands. Next, turn the piece over and examine it to see if the fabric has adhered to the entire surface. If it has not, and hand pressure will not cause the loose spots to adhere, the glue has probably dried too much in those spots. This can be remedied by pressing the surface with a hot iron and a slightly dampened pressing cloth.

Turn the work face down again, clip the corners off the unattached fabric, and fold about an inch over on the back side—gluing one side at a time. Now cut out the center, leaving sufficient material all around to fold over. Cut the fabric at the corners like a miter joint and glue down. After covering a mat place it between smooth surfaces (such as pieces of Upson board or Masonite) with the fabric protected by clean wrapping paper or waxed paper. Then place weights (such as books) on top until the glue sets.

Attaching artwork to backing with gummed paper hinges.

Using a stiff brush, apply glue evenly to the face of the mat. Place it face down on the linen (above).

Having smoothed the linen and made sure it has made contact all over, proceed to clip excess fabric at the corners and glue the edges down on the back (opposite, top).

Clip out the center, miter the corners, and glue inside edges down on the back (opposite, bottom).

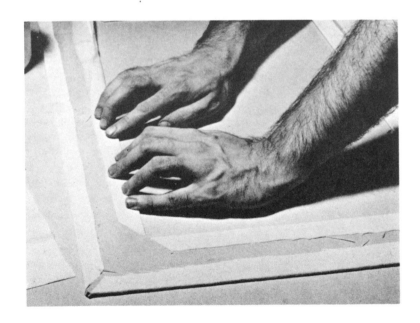

Very lightweight materials such as silk shantung or pongee are most easily used if the fabric is *not* glued to the face of the mat. Simply lay the mat face-down on the material and paste one edge of the fabric to the back of the mat. Glue the opposite edge next, stretching the fabric lightly as you work, being careful to keep the weave running in straight lines. When the four outside edges are in place, cut the center out and proceed to pull the edges in and paste them down.

Covered mats are often used as the top mat of a double-mat job. The lower mat may have a gold bevel. In double mats the window in the top mat should be at least ¼″ larger than that in the under mat. The gilt bevel on the under mat can be *leafed*. A simpler method, however, is to cover the bevel with metallic foil paper. This paper is available in art-supply stores but is the variety commonly used for gift wrapping and consists of a white paper backing to which is attached a thin coating of gold or silver foil. Cover the bevel of the mat by gluing the foil paper to it, folding it under and pasting it on the back side. Be sure to miter the corners with the mat knife. Glue the top mat to the bottom one to prevent slipping out of line in the frame.

*Mats without Windows (Drop-on Mountings)*

Occasionally a work of art cannot afford to lose even a small area around the edge where a mat would overlap. Many original prints, especially woodcuts, are executed on beautifully textured papers which have or can be given interesting frayed edges. Often antique drawings have been damaged so that matting in the usual manner is difficult because of the irregular shape of the paper. In such cases *drop-on* mountings are useful. A drop-on is simply a piece of matboard upon which the artwork is laid and attached lightly with paper hinges or dabs of library paste. When the glass is in place the work remains pressed against the mat. In the illustration on page 47 a large woodcut has been frayed around the edges by tearing the paper against a saw edge. It has been dropped on a linen-covered piece of Upson board which serves as both mat and backing.

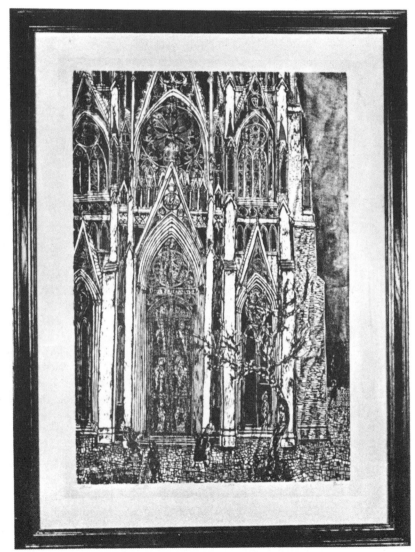

47　　　　　　　Ted Davies: *Cathedral*, 22″ x 28″ woodcut, frame and mount 5″.

# CUTTING AND JOINING THE MOLDING

## CUTTING

The *miter box* is an important tool; anyone who anticipates making more than a few picture frames should own a good one. I recommend the Stanley No. 60 pictured here.

Follow these rules when using the miter box: Cut the molding into approximate lengths with a regular right-angle cut. Then, setting the saw for the right-hand 45° angle, cut all the right-hand ends. In cutting flats, the two pieces that are to form opposite sides of a frame may be stacked on each other and cut at the same time to assure equal length. Moldings which will not stack must be registered against a stopping device so that both pieces will be the same length.

A simple method of registering is to fasten a small block of wood to the cutting table or molding runway. Push this block firmly against the end of the molding opposite the saw just after completing the cut on the first piece. Secure the block with a C clamp. When the next piece of molding is slid under the saw, make sure the end butts firmly against the block before lowering the saw. If necessary, molding may be clamped in the miter box while it is being sawed.

When cutting the molding into approximate lengths remember that you must allow for the *square* of the molding width at each end of the piece for cutting the miter joint. If you are cutting a 16″ × 20″ frame from a 3″ molding you must add twice the width of the molding— 6″—to each of the sides; your pieces must measure 22″ for the 16″ sides and 26″ for the 20″ sides—so at least an 8′ length of molding will be required to cut such a frame. Always allow a little more than the bare necessity. See the diagram on page 50.

After cutting the right-hand ends at a 45° angle, measure with the rule along the back of the rabbet to the desired length and draw a pencil mark at the point where the cut should be made. Place the molding under

48

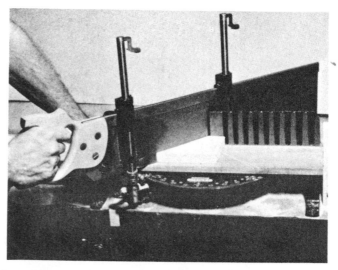

After cutting the molding into approximate lengths, cut the right-hand end of each piece to a 45° angle.

Set the saw for the left-hand angle cut and cut the left-hand ends, using a stop to assure equal length of matching pieces or by cutting two pieces at once.

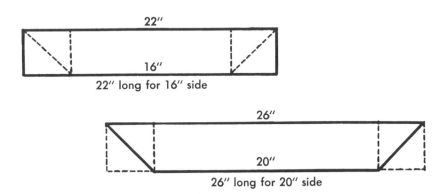

22" long for 16" side

26" long for 20" side

the saw so that the pencil mark is just clear of the kurf cut—just past the shallow cut the saw makes in the bottom of the miter box after passing through the molding. When you have made the cut the pencil mark should still be on the piece that will become the side of the frame. This is called *saving* the line, and this way none of your pieces will be cut *shy* by mistake.

## DRILLING THE NAILHOLES

A quarter-inch *electric hand drill* is also a useful tool to the picture framer. The one shown here is of the *pistol-grip* variety, with the switch in the handle. For purposes of drilling the moldings the switch has been locked in the *on* position and the handle clamped in a vise. The current is shut off and on by a cord switch. This arrangement leaves both hands free to hold and guide the molding while drilling nailholes. Drilled holes are necessary for greater ease in joining the pieces, to prevent splitting, and to act as directional guides for the nails. They should be drilled carefully with a drill bit slightly smaller in diameter than the nails.

To drill the nailholes, grasp the molding in both hands as shown, with the face up—rabbet toward you. Drill two or three holes in the right-hand end of the molding. Tilt the molding slightly back and to the left, so that when the nail enters the adjoining piece it will point more toward the bottom and back of the molding than toward the top and face. This tilt should not be extreme; the nails should go almost straight into the heart of the other piece. Having drilled all the pieces, remove the drill from the vise.

## JOINING THE MOLDING

Place one of the long sides of the molding in the vise as shown (on page 54) with the mitered end just free of the jaws. Form the habit of *always* placing the long piece in the vise and joining the short piece to it; thus you will avoid joining the wrong corners. When you have made two joints in this way they will match correctly for joining into a frame.

Apply a dab of glue to the molding in the vise. Taking the short piece in your left hand as shown, place it a little *back* of the desired position so that the hammer blow when the first nail is driven will drive

After making the right-hand cut, measure off the proper size along the back of the rabbet.

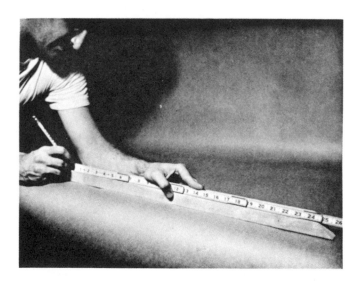

51

the molding forward into exact position. The first nail should be slightly smaller than the other two used for the corner so that it will slide easily into the hole. When this nail has been driven and the molding guided into position by pressure from the left hand and taps from the hammer, the molding will be locked in place. The other nails may then be driven in.

## TOOLS FOR JOINING

### Vise

The kind of vise needed is a common 3″ or 4″ bench vise. The one shown is a 3½″ Littlestown No. 25. The faces of the jaws have been covered with leather pads to prevent the vise jaws from marring the moldings. The pads are glued in place with contact cement and must be replaced from time to time.

### Nails

Size of nails—wire brads or finishing nails—is determined by the size of the molding. For ½″ moldings, a No. 17 or No. 18 wire brad ¾″ or 1″ long should do. For 1½″ moldings use fourpenny finishing nails. Your stock of nails should also include· No. 16 wire brads 1″ long, sixpenny, eightpenny, and tenpenny finishing nails.

### Nail Set

You should have one or two nail sets for setting the heads of the nails below the surface of the frame. Do not tap the nail set too hard. The heads of the nails should be just buried beneath the surface.

### Hammers

For joining, a carpenter's claw hammer is best. The one pictured is a 13-ounce forged-steel head. The only other hammer you will need is an upholsterer's tack hammer for *assembling* (tacking the picture into the frame).

As soon as you have driven all three nails, use the nail set to sink the heads. This allows for better finishing and also strengthens the joint.

Remove the joined corner from the vise and proceed to join the two other pieces. You now have two identical corners—if you have been careful to place the long piece in the vise and join the short one to it. Place one section in the vise. If the frame is large, have at hand a box or other object the proper height to serve as temporary support for the corner diagonally opposite the vise; this will avoid undue strain on the freshly nailed corners.

### OTHER EQUIPMENT

A pair of electrician's diagonal *wirecutters* is an important item. You will need these to cut picture wire and occasionally to pull nails.

The *picture wire* should be braided; either iron and steel, or copper. Numbers 2 and 3 will be most useful. The wire should be attached with good strong screw eyes that are not too large. On heavy frames it is best to use flat straphangers, which are attached with screws and are less likely to break or pull out under strain.

A *nailing edge* is a necessity in assembling. This may be a bar of wood permanently attached to the edge of the table or a removable piece held by C clamps. The nailing edge acts as a brace against which you rest the side of the frame into which you are driving the nails. The face against which the frame rests should be covered with leather or felt to protect finishes.

Tilt and angle of the drilled hole are important. Practice will enable you to know when both are just right.

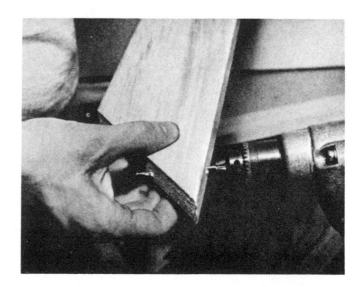

53

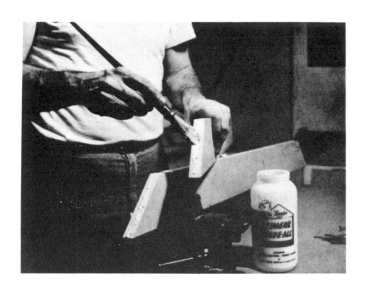

Place the long piece in the vise and apply glue to the ends that are to be joined.

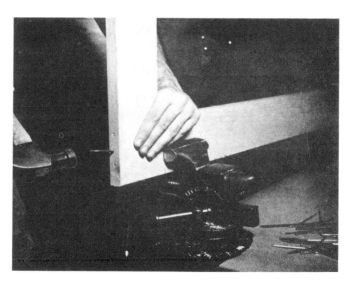

The first nail should be slightly smaller than the others so that it slips easily into the hole.

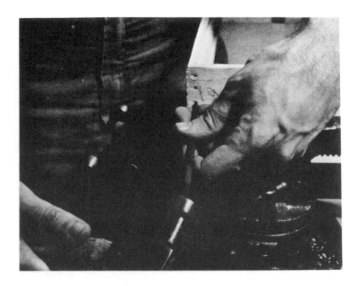

When all the nails are driven, use the nail set to sink the heads a short distance beneath the surface.

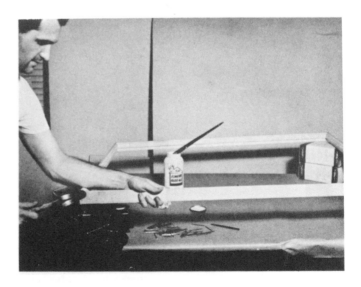

When joining the two corner sections into a frame, use a support for the corner diagonally opposite the vise to avoid strain on the fresh joints.

# GLASS AND GLASS-CUTTING

The proper glass to use is *picture glass*, which is thinner and clearer than window glass. Single-strength window glass may be used if picture glass is unavailable. Anyone who does his own picture framing will probably want to cut his own glass. One may choose, of course, to take the frames to a glazier and have them professionally fitted with panes. Glass-cutting, nevertheless, is easily mastered and the tools are simple.

Some difficulties may be overcome by making your frames conform to certain standard sizes in which glass is usually available. Many times altering the size of a mat by ¼″ will allow you to use a standard-size glass.

A few of the standard sizes are:

| | | |
|---|---|---|
| 8″ × 10″ | 16″ × 20″ | 24″ × 30″ |
| 9″ × 12″ | 18″ × 24″ | 26″ × 32″ |
| 11″ × 14″ | 20″ × 24″ | 28″ × 38″ |
| 14″ × 18″ | 22″ × 28″ | 30″ × 40″ |

Even the best glazier makes faulty cuts sometimes, so do not be discouraged if you are not successful at first. Glass should be cut on a firm, smooth surface. If your work table has irregularities, it should be surfaced with a piece of Masonite. The best type of glass-cutter for the amateur is the rotary steel wheel in a steel handle available in any hardware store. These are so inexpensive that the whole tool may be discarded when the wheel wears dull. A similar type has a wooden handle and replaceable steel wheels; this is equally satisfactory. If you keep a small amount of oil on the wheel, it will last much longer.

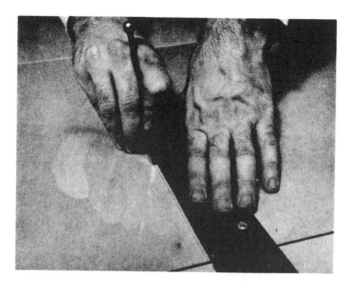

Hold the glass-cutter as shown. Apply a firm, even, not-too-hard pressure. Make the cut in one continuous action—it need not be fast.

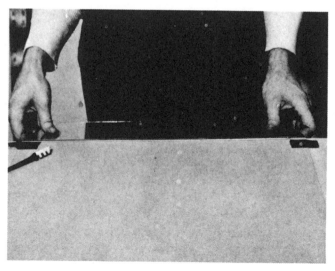

After scoring the glass with the cutter, draw it over the table edge and snap off the projecting piece.

A steel straightedge should be used as a guide for the cutter. Place a small piece of masking tape on the glass at each edge as marks for placing the straightedge. Hold the cutter between the first two fingers, as shown, applying pressure with the forefinger and thumb and, guiding with the middle finger, draw the cutter firmly and evenly over the glass with enough pressure to make an even white mark and a little burring sound. (You will soon get to know when the cutter sounds just right.) After scoring the glass, move it to the edge of the table so that the smaller section projects over and the cut at the table's edge. With fingers firmly grasping the edge of the glass, lift it half an inch or so off the table—with the far edge of the glass still resting on the table. Snap it down sharply against the table edge. The scored cut should break open. If the glass fails to break, you have not made the proper cut. It is often possible to save the glass at this point. First turn it over face down on the table. With the handle of the cutter or any other blunt instrument, tap gently along the full length of the cut. This will usually cause it to break through. If this method fails, try making a new cut on this (back) side, breaking off the glass as if it were the original cut.

Never run the cutter more than once over the same cut. Recutting a line not only ruins the cutting wheel but almost invariably also shatters the glass. If you have cut a small sliver (less than an inch), break it off with square-nosed pliers rather than your fingers.

Practice making cuts on scraps of glass until you are able to execute a full cut in one continuous action; it need not be fast. After you have developed some facility with the cutter, you should be able to cut glass directly in the frame without the steel straightedge, using only the edge of the rabbet (seen through the glass) as a guide for freehand cutting.

# MATERIALS AND METHODS FOR FINISHING

### WAX FINISHES

In considering appropriate finishes for frames, the first possibility is utilization of the natural color and grain of the wood from which the molding is made. Frames of walnut or chestnut are often given a wax finish, which brings out the grain and deepens the color. First prepare the surface by sandpapering all rough spots and rubbing the entire face down to a smooth surface with steel wool. Wipe the wood with a rag to remove dust. Then apply a thin coat of white shellac (with a little alcohol added) to seal the grain. If you wish to darken the wood slightly, add a small amount of orange shellac to the white. After the shellac coating is thoroughly dry, rub it down with fine steel wool until the surface is smooth. Apply a generous coating of white paste wax with a rag and buff to a satiny gloss. Do not use a heavy coat of shellac; very shiny moldings tend to look cheap.

Even the light-colored woods such as basswood, poplar, and birch —from which many picture-frame moldings are made—will look quite good with only a wax finish. This is particularly true of small-size moldings used to frame drawings and watercolors.

### STAIN FINISHES

The light wood can be toned to darker shades with oil stains. Thin the oil stain with turpentine until you are able to achieve the desired shade.

Apply the stain with a brush or rag; wipe off any excess with a dry rag—do not allow stain to remain on the surface. When the stain has dried, apply a coat of shellac. Rub this coat down with steel wool also, and finish with a waxing as described above.

## CASEIN PAINT

Casein paints are among the most useful materials for frame finishing. Luminall L-400 white has many uses. It serves as substitute for *gesso* (the hot glue and whiting mixture used by professionals); thinned with water and toned by the addition of casein colors or Luminall Fresco colors, it makes an excellent antiquing solution. Although there are many other brands of casein housepaints available, Luminall is probably the best for framing uses. Do not buy latex-base paints merely because they too are water soluble. Latex-base paints do not function in the same manner as caseins. They tend to roll up when steel-wooled and to peel when intermixed with layers of turpentine, oil, and shellac.

## ANTIQUE WHITE

Luminall white may be thinned with water for varying effects. To make a simple toned or antique-white finish, paint the entire visible portion of the frame with Luminall thinned to the consistency of thick cream. When this has dried, give it a second coat. Use a bristle brush and have the paint sufficiently thick for the impression of the bristles to make a texture in the surface. Be sure to run the strokes in long lines the full length of the side of the frame. Whatever pattern you create will be much more evident when the frame is antiqued. Let the paint dry thoroughly.

Next, prepare an *antiquing solution.* A simple one can be made from turpentine and oil color or japan color in very thin solution—it should really be just tinted turpentine. Use burnt umber with a touch of black to make a pleasing gray-buff. Saturate the frame with this mixture,

Apply turpentine and japan-color antiquing solution liberally over the white Luminall surface.

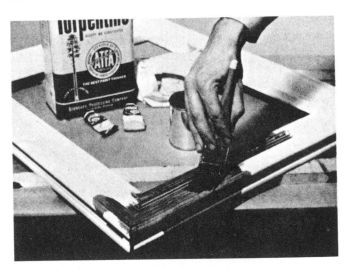

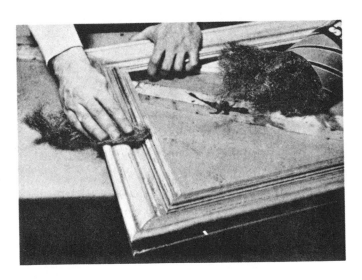

Rub the antiquing off quickly with rags; follow by a rubbing with a coarse steel wool to expose the grained effect.

applying it generously with a rag or brush. Follow immediately with a dry rag to wipe off the excess, working quickly around the frame until the moisture disappears. This should leave the frame tinted a soft gray or brown. If the effect is uneven, you are not using enough of the turpentine mixture—wet it down and rub it dry again to even the tone. Using coarse steel wool (No. 3), rub the frame vigorously. The steel wool removes the stain from the ridges, exposing white paint, and leaves it in the depressions, creating a pleasing grained effect.

## RUBBED FINISHES

Rubbed white, rubbed gray, and other rubbed color finishes are very popular. This effect usually looks best on wood with some grain and color such as chestnut. The most simple method is to thin Luminall with water until it is quite watery. Tint it to the desired shade with Luminall Fresco colors or casein colors. Paint a thin coat over the frame and wipe it off gently with a damp cloth—the idea is to leave a semitransparent coating. When this paint dries it will be several shades lighter than when wet, so allow for this when mixing the color. After the paint dries, rub the surface with steel wool. This will remove the paint from the high points of the grain and leave it in the deep parts. When done with white this finish is sometimes called *limed*. After the steel-wool rubbing apply a light coat of white paste wax to eliminate the chalky effect.

## DRIFTWOOD FINISHES

Driftwood effects are among the most popular of all finishes. They can be toned to complement almost any picture and they do not show wear. Many wide scoop shapes and reverse moldings are finished this way. Often a platform frame has a driftwood back with a gold or white top. Driftwood effects can be produced on any molding surface, but wormy chestnut is ideal. One method is to score the surface with a sharp tool such as a beer-can opener or an icepick. Dent the frame here and there with a hammer and roughen the edges with a wood rasp. Use a dark walnut stain and coat the entire frame. When the stain is dry, coat with white shellac. Do not use steel wool at this point. Pass over the frame with a watery gray mixture of Luminall (as in the rubbed finishes). Wipe off excess with a damp cloth and allow the paint to dry. Steel-wool and sandpaper the surface to expose various layers of wood, stain, or antiquing. After this you may spatter the surface with a little oil or japan color in turpentine, using a toothbrush and a stick.

There is of course no limit to the number of coatings, stainings, rubbings, and scrapings you may use to achieve a desired effect. You will avoid difficulties if you make it a practice to separate the various layers of your finish with coats of shellac to prevent *bleeding* and running.

Some framers like to add sparkle to their toned finishes by dry-brushing bronze or aluminum powder on the high points. This can be done with shellac or bronzing liquid by simply tapping the tips of a stiff-bristle brush and dabbing it in some of the powder spilled out on a paper. Whisk the brush lightly where you desire the sheen, but avoid overdoing any metallic effects.

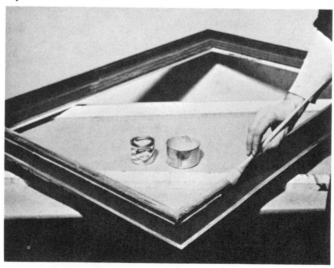

Gold size being applied (with a little yellow oil color added to make it easy to see spots you have missed).

## METAL LEAFING

Gold and silver effects achieved with actual thin sheets of metal applied to the frame surface, a process known as *leafing*, are an important operation in picture framing. The equipment is simple and inexpensive. *Metal leaf* is the term used for the imitation gold leaf (actually bronze). The best grades come from Germany and Italy and the color is designated by numbers. For our purposes No. 2½ will do very well. It comes in books, interleaved between tissue. The sheets are about 5½″ square. A book contains twenty-five sheets, with twenty books to a pack. Imitation silver is aluminum leaf.

You will need a rather soft bristle brush about 2″ wide for patting the leaf into place. Also necessary are scissors, soft rags, cotton batting or velvet, shellac, and gold size (Hastings Quick Size).

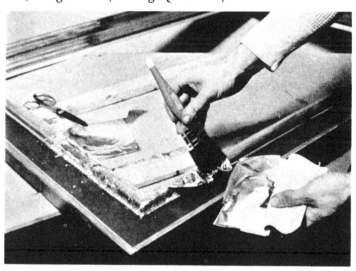

Lay the leaf from the book, using a bristle brush to tap it gently into place.

The surface to receive leaf must first be prepared as though for a finish coat of paint. A good method, which gives an effect of real gold-leaf work, begins by painting the molding with red Luminall. This red should be a mixed color made of burnt sienna or Venetian red mixed with a little pure red. The idea is to simulate the red-clay base used under real gold work. When the red paint is dry, rub it down with steel wool to a smooth surface. Remember that the gold surface will be no smoother than the base coat. Add two coats of shellac so that the surface is perfectly sealed. The next step is to apply a coat of size to serve as adherent for the leaf. Hasting's Quick Size is best for most jobs. You may add a small amount of chrome-yellow oil color to the size to give it a milky-yellow color that will enable you to see what parts you have covered. Brush the size out to a thin, even coat. Do not go back over areas already covered. *Never* thin the size with turpentine. Because old size decomposes, buy the smallest containers available and replace them when necessary.

The size is really a varnish and the principle of leafing is to let the size dry until it is tacky but no longer wet before laying the leaf on it. Let the size dry for about an hour. Then test it with the bent knuckle of your finger to see if it has reached its proper *tack*. If the knuckle pulls away without sticking but makes a slight *tick*-sound, the size is right for laying the leaf. Do not lay the leaf in wet size, but do not let it dry beyond its proper tack period or the leaf will not stick at all. Between one and three hours after applying the size should be the proper time for laying the leaf.

On small moldings, the book of leaf can be cut in half and you can lay half sheets. For larger moldings, use full sheets. Lay the sheet of leaf on the tacky surface, patting it in place with the soft wide brush. Work all around the frame as quickly as possible, laying the leaf generously, overlapping each sheet at least ¼". Then go around again with the brush, patting, tapping, brushing away some of the excess, and adding bits of leaf where you have missed. Experience will teach you just how much brushing is necessary at this stage. Set the frame aside and let it dry at least eight hours.

The next step is to brush off all excess leaf. Rub the entire surface with a soft cloth, cotton batting, or a piece of velvet. Apply a thin coat of white shellac with a little orange shellac added for color. This is necessary whether or not you intend to antique over the leaf because metal leaf corrodes on contact with air.

Many aluminum leaf jobs have the *coves*, or deep parts, coated with *gold lacquer* on top of the shellac to simulate the golden glow of antique silver and avoid the raw, tin appearance of the leaf.

Many metal-leaf finishes may be antiqued very simply by going over them with a mixture of turpentine and oil or japan colors mixed to the desired hue. This mixture is then wiped off with a soft cloth. The frame may be *flyspecked* by flicking umber or black japan color and turpentine from a toothbrush pushed against a straightedge. Many framers dust the antiqued frame with *rotten stone* (artificial dust) to remove any tackiness and add to the antique effect.

The black back or side is a classic finish for many styles of frames with metal-leafed faces. The black should not be painted until after the leaf has been shellacked. The best paint for this purpose is lampblack in japan.

# ASSEMBLING

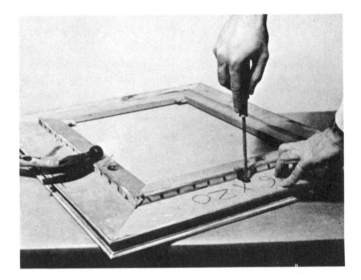

Two methods for attaching a canvas in the frame: (*left*) a nail through the stretcher; (*right*) an angle clamp screwed into place.

The process of getting the artwork into the completed frame is known as *assembling*. For canvases and panels the procedure is very simple. In most cases the frame has a rabbet and the picture is secured in place by laying it in position from the back of the frame and fastening it with nails. A panel usually requires four or five 1″ wire brads along each side. The canvas stretcher has a small raised edge about ¼″ wide; nails (fourpenny or sixpenny finishing nails) are driven just inside this ridge and angled through the stretcher into the rabbet. This angled nailing through the stretcher not only locks the picture in place but is necessary in most cases because the thickness of the stretcher protrudes beyond the depth of the rabbet. Some artists prefer not to pierce their stretchers. In this case spring turnbuttons may be used, two to the side. This is handy for quick removal of a canvas from a frame. Others prefer to screw small angle clamps to the stretcher and to the frame.

Assembling frames with glass requires a few more steps. First the glass must be washed. The best cleaner is plain water. Dampen a soft cloth and rub one side of the glass vigorously. Follow up with a dry cloth, rubbing and polishing until clean. Turn the glass over and repeat the operation. If the glass is especially dirty, a touch of ammonia in the water will help. Do *not* use commercial glass cleaners—many of these leave a chemical film on the glass. Work on clean paper covering a flat table. Lay the matted artwork or other piece being framed face-down on the clean glass. Put the backing board in place and turn the entire unit over to examine the front for fingermarks or pieces of lint or trash caught between

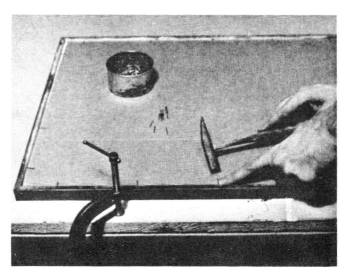

With the frame resting against the nailing edge, press down on the backing and drive wire brads 4 to 5 inches apart.

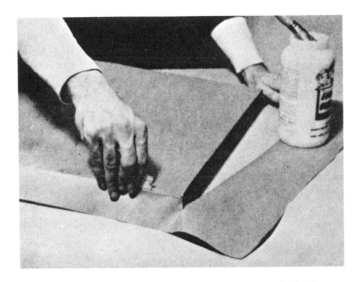

Using a single-edge razor blade, trim the paper on the back.

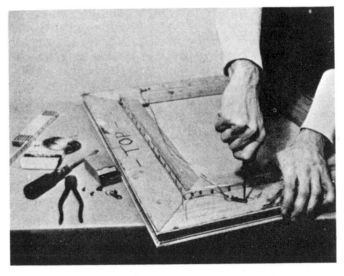

Use an awl to punch starting holes for screws or **screw eyes**.

the glass and the picture. Put the frame in position and turn the whole unit upside down again. With the edge of the frame resting against the nailing edge on the table, proceed to drive wire brads about ¼″ into the back of the rabbet—pressing down on the backing at the same time to assure a tight fit. Use four to ten nails per side. Nail opposite sides alternately.

After nailing, seal the back of the frame against dust. Use a sheet of ordinary wrapping paper a little larger than the frame. Dampen the paper lightly with a sponge and roll it into a loose roll until you have applied glue to the frame (Elmer's Glue-all is good for this). Brush it all around the back of the frame and lay the damp wrapping paper (40-lb. kraft is good) in place. Go around the edges with your fingers, pressing the paper into the glue until it holds. Next, using a single-edge razor blade, cut the excess paper away from the edge. Using your middle finger as a guide, let the blade ride just inside the edge of the molding. When the paper dries it will draw taut. The piece is now ready for screw eyes and wire. Do not place the screw eyes more than one third down from the top of the frame. If they are too low they will cause the picture to tip forward.

Hanging pictures deserves passing mention. Most things look best when hung at normal eye level of a standing adult; the most common mistake of the layman is hanging things too high. Picture hooks or finishing nails are equally good for hanging. If two nails or hooks are used, spaced 4″ to 6″ apart, the picture will not seesaw out of position. In plaster walls it is best to drill holes for the nails. Paste-on hangers are not safe.

# PASSE PARTOUT

*Passe partout* is an inexpensive method for presentation of works of art, a kind of temporary framing often used for exhibition purposes when large numbers of things must be displayed. *Passe partout* involves glass, mat, and backing (with hangers attached) held together by strips of tape binding the edges.

Special tapes are available in art-supply stores, but gummed-paper tape or cloth adhesive may be used. Determine the size and cut your mat, glass, and backing as you would for a permanent framing job. Attach the artwork and clean the glass. Before putting the backing in place, attach the hangers (called *passe partout rings*). Pierce the chipboard backing and push the rings through; paste the ends down and cover them with squares of paper tape. Now put the backing in place and line up all edges as evenly as possible. Leave one edge of this stack projecting slightly over

Pierce the backing with a mat knife and pass the hanger rings through.

the table edge. Lay the steel straightedge about ¼″ inside this edge. The straightedge is to serve as a guide for pasting the tape and may be held in place with a C clamp if desired. Having cut the tape in pieces about 1″ longer than the sides to be taped, moisten it and paste it to the glass; fold it down and under, pasting it to the back. Turn the whole unit carefully and do the opposite side. Trim the excess at the ends before pasting the adjoining sides. Do not lap the tape over the glass face more than ¼″. This neat little line of tape has a good appearance and is surprisingly strong.

When all the tapes are in place a wire may be run between the rings on the back for hanging.

Bind the edges carefully and neatly; do opposite sides alternately. Finish corners by trimming excess tape with razor blade. Attach picture wire between the rings. Robert Moore: *Drawing*, 11″ x 14″, mat and tape 2″ x 2½″.

# SHADOW BOXES

*Shadow boxes* are used primarily to frame collages, reliefs, jewelry, or any delicate three-dimensional object. There are two kinds: the *double frame* and the *lined box*. The *double frame* is made by placing one frame inside another, the glass held between the frames and the depth of the box created by the height of the inner frame. In the illustration on page 74 a 1″ gold scoop frame is used inside a walnut reverse. The object is mounted on a velvet-covered board.

The lined-box style is made with only one frame. It must be of a molding with sufficient depth inside the rabbet to accommodate the glass, the object, and the backing. First place the glass in the frame and measure the remaining depth. Cut strips of double-thick matboard wide enough to reach from the glass to within about ¼″ of the back. These are then covered with the same fabric used to cover the mounting board and are glued in place around the inside of the frame, forming walls which hold the glass in place on the front and create a rabbet at the back to receive the mounting board.

The object should naturally be securely attached to the mounting board. This may be done with glue or by sewing it in place with wires or threads piercing the board, depending on the nature of the piece.

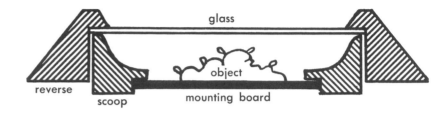

glass

reverse

scoop

object

mounting board

Double-frame shadow box. Cross-sectional diagram is shown above.

# WET MOUNTING

Wet mounting of art reproductions is relatively simple, since reproductions are printed on heavy stock with inks that are not water-soluble. Original artwork, on the other hand, presents many individual problems. If the work uses water-soluble inks or colors, it must be *fixed* before starting to mount. A good product for this purpose is Krylon Crystal Clear Spray. If the paper is very lightweight or porous it may be best not to dampen it. Apply the paste to the mounting board and lay the work on it. For mounting heavier papers apply the paste to the back of the piece.

The process shown here is the mounting of an art reproduction. The paste is ordinary wallpaper wheat paste. The mounting board is 3⁄16″ Upson board. Semitransparent papers should be mounted on white double-thick matboard. Such pieces as original drawings, which are to be framed under glass, need no more than matboard or chipboard for mounting; works that are to be sprayed with a protective coating and framed without glass need at least the 3⁄16″ Upson board. Masonite is less satisfactory for mounting because its oiled surface does not absorb paste.

Cut two sheets of heavy kraft paper 4″ to 6″ larger than the piece to be mounted. Cut the Upson board at least 2″ larger than the size of the piece (in both directions). When wet, many papers stretch considerably. For this reason you should have room on the mounting board to accommodate the stretch. Always do your mounting *before* making the frame.

With the work facing down on one of the pieces of kraft paper, dampen the entire back with a sponge soaked in clean water. Keep going over the paper with the wet sponge until the paper becomes limp and lies flat. Roll the piece, together with the kraft paper, into a loose roll. Lay it aside until you are ready to apply the paste. If you are mounting three or four pieces, do all the wetting down at once. Unroll the artwork and apply paste to the back. Use a large brush; try not to leave any heavy

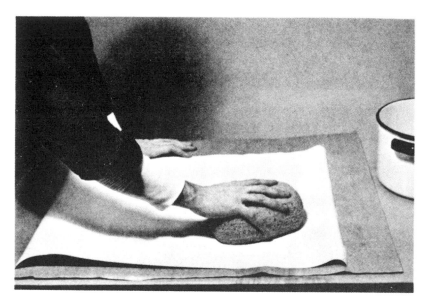

Wet the back of the print, using clean water and sponge.

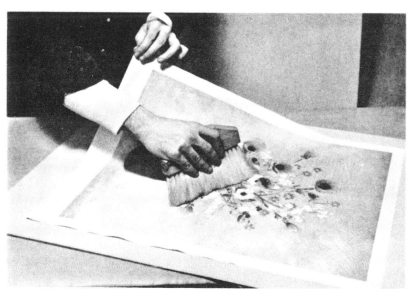

Lift the corner and brush from the center to smooth out air pockets.

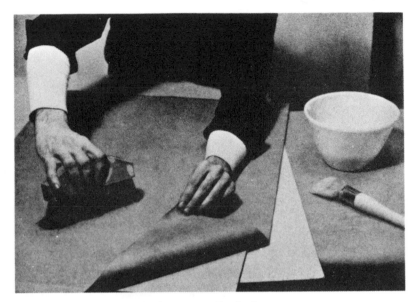

Countermount by pasting kraft paper on the back.

ridges of paste. The secret of good mounting is to use as little paste as possible to accomplish the job. Lift the paper and position it on the mounting board. Starting at the center and working toward the corners, smooth the paper to remove all air bubbles. Lift one corner and smooth it down from the center using a dry cloth or wallpaper brush. Repeat on all four corners. Turn the mounted piece face-down on the dry sheet of kraft paper and, using the dampened piece which was rolled with the work, *countermount*—paste the kraft paper to the back side of the board in the same manner you pasted the picture to the front. When drying the two papers pull against each other to minimize warping. Leaving the clean, dry piece of kraft paper to protect it, place the mounted work between two smooth surfaces and apply weights to it while it is drying. It should remain under pressure about a day. Then allow the piece to lie flat on a table for several days, exposed to the air.

When completely dry, any piece to be framed without glass should be given a protective coating. Krylon Crystal-Clear Spray is best for this purpose. Spray on several coats, but do not *flood* the surface. Mounted pieces look best when not too shiny. After it is sprayed, the piece should be cut to size, using a T square and straightedge.

# FRAMING A PIECE
# UNDER GLASS

Measure for the mat and calculate the size of the frame.

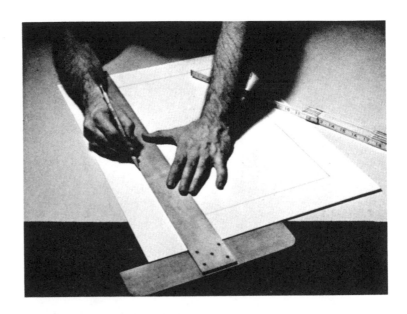

Lay out the opening, using the T square and rule.

Cut the mat, using a steel straightedge and mat knife.

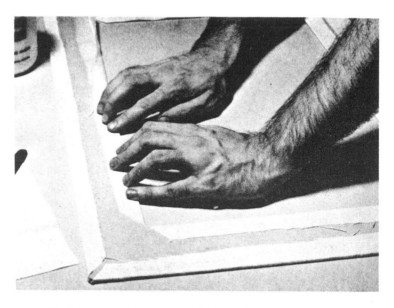

Cover the mat with linen, using glue as described in the section on covered mats.

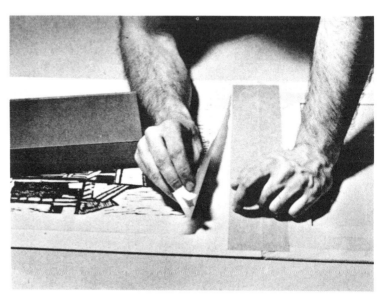

Attach the artwork, using small gummed paper hinges.

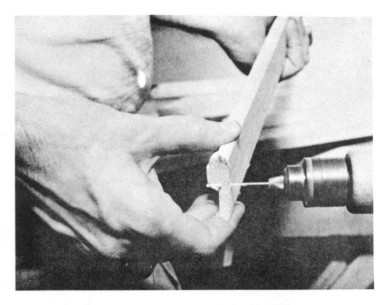

Having cut the frame to the proper size, drill the nailholes for joining.

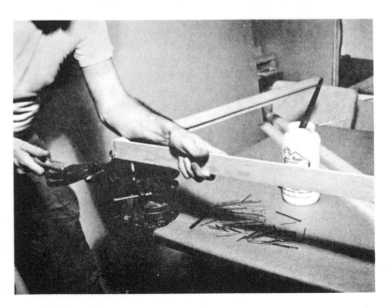

Join the frame and allow glue to set.

Apply walnut oil stain and rub off with rag. Apply coat of shellac when stain is dry.

Apply Luminall antiquing with a brush and wipe off with a damp cloth.

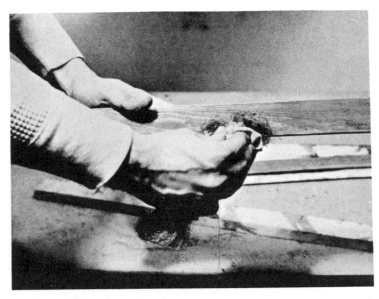

When the antiquing is thoroughly dry, rub with steel wool to expose the stained wood. A light waxing will eliminate chalkiness.

Cut the glass to size. Do not make the fit too tight.

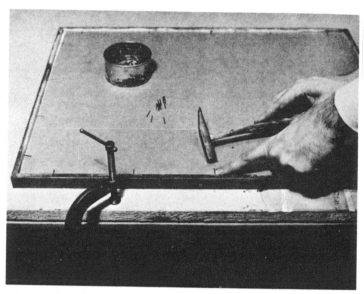

Wash and dry glass, place work in frame with backing. Nail in place with No. 18 wire brads.

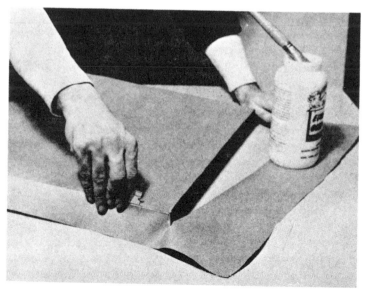

Apply glue around edge, press dampened kraft paper in place. Trim away excess with razor blade.

Place picture wire between screw eyes for hanging, and the job is finished.
Ted Davies: *El Station*, 12″ x 16″ woodcut, mat and frame 3½″.

# FRAMING A CANVAS

Measure the canvas and test it for squareness with a **T** square. Decide what style of frame or molding to use. For this job, a center-panel style was chosen.

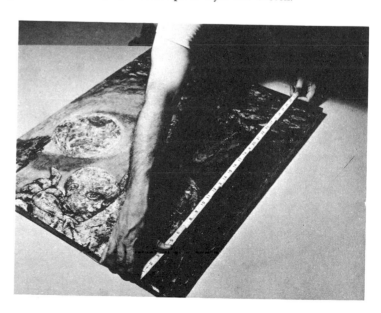

Cut the frame liner with the usual ¼″ allowance, then cut the flat molding for the frame.

Flats may be joined in vertical position in the vise, as shown.

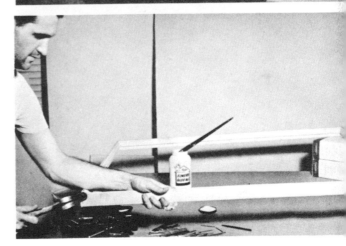

Joining the outer frame in horizontal position.

Apply glue to the top molding and position it on the flat. Attach with wire brads and set the heads. (Remember that this molding will project over the edge of the flat to form a rabbet.)

After attaching the outer-edge molding in the same manner, give the entire frame a coat of red Luminall as a base for leafing.

When the red is dry, rub it with steel wool and apply two coats of shellac. Apply gold size to inner and outer moldings.

Lay the leaf when the size has reached its proper tack. Allow time for drying, then coat with shellac.

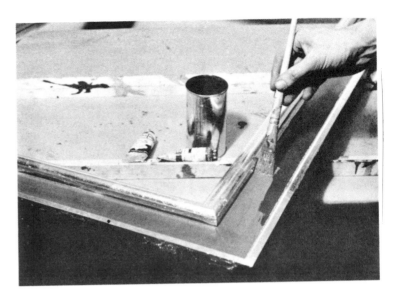

The color tone in the center panel should be related to the color in the painting. Here oil color and japan color were mixed to two hues which were applied separately with a coat of shellac between.

Having sealed the entire surface with shellac, apply Luminall antique (mixed to a suitable gray) and wipe off with a damp cloth. When the antique is thoroughly dry, rub with coarse steel wool to allow the various layers to show. The metal leaf also is scratched to expose the red underneath. Wipe the dust from the frame and spatter with flecks of color and black or dark-brown *flyspecks*. Nail the linen-covered liner into the finished frame. Fasten the canvas in place, and attach hangers and wire for hanging. This is an example of a modern use of the center-panel frame style.

Harry Sternberg: *Radiation*, 24″ x 30″ canvas, frame and liner 6½″. Courtesy A.C.A. Gallery.

# GLOSSARY

**Allowance.** Extra space inside a picture frame to accommodate the panel or canvas with ease.

**Antique, antiquing.** Effect of artificial age created in the finishing of a frame by applying a special solution and sometimes using techniques such as **distressing**.

**Antique silver.** A finish usually made by leafing with aluminum leaf, coating in part with gold lacquer or orange shellac, and sprinkling with flyspecks.

**Antique white.** A finish usually made by painting solid white, then discoloring with an antiquing solution.

**Basswood.** The most common picture-frame molding material; the wood of the linden tree.

**Canvas.** The already-painted support of the artist's picture; a cloth stretched on a wooden frame called a **stretcher**. (In this book the term is also used to refer to an oil painting.)

**Center-panel.** Frame style in which a flat molding is bounded on both sides by raised ornamental moldings.

**Chipboard.** Gray pulp cardboard, used for picture backing.

**Countermount.** To paste a paper on the reverse side of a mounting board to cause stress opposing that caused by the mounted work.

**Cove.** Any inner recess or hollowed-out part in a molding.

**Distressing.** Artificial wear or damage given the finish of a frame for antique effect.

**Driftwood.** Coarsely distressed and antiqued effects on moldings; artificial weathering.

**Drop-on.** Term used for matting without an opening; mounting of work on top of the mat.

**Flat.** Simple plank or plain molding with no ornamental surface.

**Flyspecks.** Small black or dark-brown spots flecked onto a finish as part of the antique effect.

**Folder mat.** Hinged mat; mat with a backing attached by means of a paper-tape hinge.

**Gold lacquer.** Transparent amber japan varnish used over aluminum leaf to imitate antique silver. Orange shellac is used as a substitute.

**Graffito.** Painted decoration, usually geometric or floral, over a leafed surface. Black is most common. Small lines are often scratched through the paint to expose gold or silver underneath.

**Hangers.** Loops or rings of steel attached to a steel strap which may be screwed to the back of a frame for attaching picture wire. A better device than screw eyes.

**Insert.** Another term for **liner**; the inner frame of a multiple frame.

**Japan color.** Color named for the medium in which it is ground: japan lacquer. These paints dry more rapidly than oils and are generally available in the same pigments.

**Kraft paper.** Brown paper used for wrapping paper, paper tape, bags.

**Leafing.** Process of covering with gold or metal leaf.

**Liner.** Frame within a frame; usually flat or beveled, often covered with fabric.

**Mat.** Border area between picture and actual frame; usually paper or board, often covered with fabric.

**Matboard.** Heavy paper or cardboard made for mats. Available in art-supply stores in single and double thickness.

**Mat knife.** Sharp straight knife with a pointed blade and one sharp edge; many have replaceable or extendable blades; used to cut mats, must be kept very sharp.

**Metal leaf.** Bronze composition imitation of gold leaf; also used to refer to aluminum leaf and other compositions.

**Miter.** The common line on which two intersecting members meet (the bisection of the angle): in picture framing almost always a 45° angle; to cut the angle necessary to make a miter joint.

**Miter box.** Device used to hold molding and saw in proper position for cutting a miter.

**Miter joint.** Union formed by two pieces of molding or other material cut with mitered ends.

**Mount.** Kind of mat or setting for small objects, especially those with high relief or difficult shapes; to place an object in its mount.

**Oil color.** Pigments ground in oil, commonly used by artists; cheaper grade used by house-painters, sometimes called **tinting color.**

**Panel.** Rigid support for a picture, usually made of wood, pressed wood, or composition board; sometimes canvas-covered (**canvasboard**); sometimes used to refer to the flat portion of a picture frame.

**Passe partout.** Method of framing in which the glass, mat, and back are held together by strips of tape pasted over the edges. The picture is hung by means of rings that are passed through the backing.

**Pebbleboard.** Matboard with a textured finish consisting of small rounded bumps and indentations.

**Platform.** Style of framing consisting of a **top molding**, containing the picture, mounted on a flat back panel.

**Rabbet.** Groove along the inside edge of a picture frame.

**Railroad.** Style of framing with a flat center panel and two more or less equal raised moldings binding the edges.

**Reverse.** Style of molding which recedes from the picture back to the wall, one in which the picture is projected from the wall almost the full height of the molding.

**Rotten stone.** Dry powder available wherever dry colors are sold; used as an imitation dust.

**Scoop.** Molding with a hollowed-out face, presenting a regular C curve; cove molding.

**Screw eyes.** Small steel or iron loops at the head on a screw; used to attach the hanging wire on the back of frames.

**Shadow box.** Framing style in which there is considerable space between glass and backing; used for framing three-dimensional objects.

**Sight-size.** Measurement of the actual visible picture opening in a frame, made along the edge of the lip of the rabbet.

**Size (gold size).** Adherent used to attach gold or metal leaf to a surface; in this book **quick size** (a japan varnish) only is discussed.

**Stretcher.** Wooden frame on which the canvas for a painting is tacked to make it taut.

**Stripping.** Slat used in lieu of an actual frame, usually simply tacked to the canvas stretcher and seldom more than ⅜" wide by 1" or 1½" deep.

**Tack.** Quality of drying gold size that has reached the stage proper for gilding—dry enough not to be picked up by a finger but fresh enough to cause the leaf to adhere.

**Top molding.** Molding attached to the top of a flat, especially in the platform and center-panel styles.

**Wet mounting.** Pasting artwork or reproductions with water-soluble paste to a stiff support.

**Wormy chestnut.** Natural chestnut wood which has been riddled by worms while standing dead in the forest, widely used for picture-frame moldings.

## ABOUT THE AUTHOR

Max Hyder was born in Asheville, North Carolina, and grew up in Bedford, Indiana. Largely self-taught, he studied art briefly at John Herron Art Institute in Indianapolis and at the Art Institute in Chicago. Mr. Hyder has served as a cook in the United States Navy, worked for a church decorating concern in Chicago, and lived for two years in a Benedictine monastery in Wisconsin. He is the creator of Sabina figurines and is now the proprietor of his own small picture framing shop in lower Manhattan.

## ABOUT THE PHOTOGRAPHER

Ted Davies is an artist-photographer who lives and works in New York. He is best known for his graphic works, especially his woodcuts, some of which appear in this book and in *Woodcuts* by Harry Sternberg, another book in the Pitman Dollar Art Series.

# Date Due

OCT 21 2006